IRONCLAD JOURNEY

The Unbreakable Strength to Keep Moving Forward

Dave Miller

Published by
StarksNest Publishing
A division of Olive Tree Resources, Inc.
P.O. Box 1031
New Albany, IN 47151
www.olivetreepartner.com

Book Cover by Morgan Miller

ISBN 9798690494322

Printed in the United States

INTRODUCTION

It started as a dream when I was young. I remember watching the Ironman world championship on TV. What would it take to push your body that far? An Ironman triathlon consists of a 2.4-mile swim, 112-mile bike and a 26.2-mile run. Total distance 140.6 miles with 16 hours to complete the race.

Fast forward about 30 years, I'm married with two kids. Our youngest is one month away from entering college. My wife and I are starting to plan what we're going to do as "empty nesters".

On July 1, 2017, our lives changed forever. I was on a training ride and lost control of my bike, hitting a car. I broke my neck, back, and nose. I'm now a quadriplegic. Paralyzed from the neck down.

I believe my endurance training and the mindset it takes to be a triathlete has helped in my recovery. Your mind can be your friend or your biggest enemy.

I hope this book inspires people to not give up. Life can change in a second. I was given a second chance, and I want to help others who are struggling to keep moving forward.

TABLE OF CONTENT

Introduction

Dave's Unbreakable Strength Quotes
Pages 90-120

Dave running to the finish line excited and
giving Drake a fist pump.

Encouragement and support along the way can make all the difference.

CHAPTER ONE
The Competitive Mind

I grew up in a small town in northern Indiana. It is a small town with a big heart. At that time, it was mainly a manufacturing area. Everything from auto parts to conveyor systems were manufactured there. It had a small one screen movie theater and a drive-in theater. A fancy night out for dinner would be at Ponderosa Steak House. We went to church twice on Sunday and on Wednesday night. No excuses! I am the youngest of six kids. We were a split family. I lived full-time with my mom, stepdad, sister, stepbrother, and stepsister. My dad had also remarried. I would see him every Wednesday and every other weekend. My stepmom had two kids - a daughter and a son. We all got along very well. Of course, we all had our days.

Most days were spent playing outside. Hide and seek, baseball, and riding bikes took up most of our time during summer break. I've never been very athletic. But if you wanted to be part of the crowd, you had to learn to hold your own. I played a few organized sports as a kid, but nothing stuck out as being the one. I really enjoyed being out on my bike. I was never the fastest, but I seemed to have endurance. We would ride our bikes everywhere. We had very few restrictions on where we could and couldn't go. Riding up to the local community college and playing basketball in their old gym is a great memory. We found an old gymnastics springboard and used it so we could dunk it!

As I got older my love for bikes never stopped. I thought I made the big leagues when I had saved enough money for a Schwinn World Sport. I'll never forget the day I picked it up from the shop. I paid $175 for it. It was maroon with silver lettering. I really thought it was the greatest thing ever. I was very proud knowing I had worked and saved my own money for my new ride. My stepbrother and I would pull a lawnmower around town behind our bikes. One of us would carry the weed eater and gas can. We would charge five dollars per yard. This was a great summer gig!

As I look back at growing up, we were always competing. My stepbrother and I were always trying to outdo each other. Who could punch the hardest, pitch the fastest, and who could pick on my sister the most? I remember we teased her terribly. We taped her up in a cardboard box and left her in the bed of a pickup truck. We held her down and acted like we were going to spit in her face. We spit at her feet to make her dance. We always reminded her we were making her tough.

My love for bikes soon turned to cars when the teenage years began. To save money for a car I started working at the local airport mowing grass and fueling airplanes. This was the beginning of a new passion for me. Unfortunately, the airport didn't pay very well so I took a job at the local Dairy Queen. After a few months, I finally had the money for my first car. It was a 1981 Ford Mustang turbo. I continued working in restaurants until I graduated high school. My passion for airplanes was still present. My best friend's family had their own airplane, and he was a pilot. We would fly everywhere! We would fly to different airports in the area for dinner. Even though I never thought about it, we were always competing. We met in middle school band. We shared first chair trombone through our sophomore year. He was destined to fly for the airlines. I didn't have the eyesight to fly so I chose to go for air traffic control.

I spent the next couple years trying to get into ATC (Air Traffic Control) School in Oklahoma City. I tried a couple times but never made the cut. I was working the ramp and ticket counter for an airline and always talked to dispatchers. I had never heard of that job, but it sounded interesting. One of the dispatchers told me it was the closest thing to ATC and flying that you could get. I did my research on schools and with a big nudge from my girlfriend (now wife) I went to South Florida to Sheffield School of Aeronautics. I was finished with school in February of 1992. I was fortunate to start with an airline the next month. I was 22 years old. Minimum age to hold the license for the job is 23.

In my interview, the manager asked where I wanted to be in five years. I told him I wanted to be in his seat. He said, "with an attitude like that a major airline would bring you on within three years." He was correct! In September of 1994, my wife and I moved to Louisville, Kentucky. I was fortunate enough to land my dream job at 25. My original plan was to be at a major airline by the time I was 40. During my career I've always wanted to be "that guy." Go to Dave if you have a question. Go to Dave, he's always willing to help.

My competitive mind has evolved over time and I never really realized it. From family to friends now coworkers this competitiveness had set in.

Competitive drive can push you to levels you didn't know you could reach.

CHAPTER TWO
Building Iron Strength

When Stacy and I moved to Louisville, we lived in a tiny one-bedroom apartment on the third floor. I was working third shift and thought I needed to stay in shape since I was killing my body working nights. I took up running. I found out very quickly I couldn't make it very far. I found a training program called "Couch to 5k." If you followed the program, it would build your endurance to run a 5k (3.1 miles) in 30 minutes. While following that program I started talking to guys at work. They told me about the "Triple Crown of Running". Living in Louisville, everything is centered around horse racing, more specifically The Kentucky Derby.

The Triple Crown of Running consists of a 5k (3.1m), 10k (6.2m) and a mini marathon (13.1m).

I ended up signing up for the races. I was consistently running for 30 minutes but no longer. After the 5k my friends said, "if you can run a 5k, you can run a 10k". I didn't believe them, but I stuck to running three to four days per week and I completed the 10k. The mini was a different scenario. I believe there was about three weeks until that race. I pushed myself to be ready for the race. One thing that was very intimidating to me was the course went through a park that was very hilly. I was used to running on very flat streets. Race morning, I was literally sick. Thank goodness for port-a-pots at the start line. I finished the race and remembered thinking, there is no way I could turn around and run this course backward to complete a marathon. My wife, Stacy and our 8-month-old daughter, Morgan were waiting just prior to the finish line. I carried Morgan across the finish line that day.

Let's jump ahead a few years to 2007. Stacy and I have two small children. They are starting to compete in their respective sports. Our evenings and weekends are now filled with practice and traveling the tri-state area going to their events. Morgan was a competitive soccer player. She played through her Sophomore year in college. Drake was a competitive swimmer for over 11 years. They were busy year around.

Some friends from work and I signed up for our first triathlon. It was a sprint distance. It consisted of an 800-yard swim, 15-mile bike and a 5k (3.1m) run. I was not prepared for the swim at all. Thank goodness it was in a pool. I literally walked most of that swim. I was on a bike I borrowed from my brother-in-law. After that race, my dream of Ironman was alive again. Running events and triathlons aren't much of a spectator sport. Stacy didn't attend very many of the races because of that fact. She was always very supportive of what I was training for. Also, while watching Ironman on TV a participant lost control of her body function and had waste running down her legs. She said, "I don't want to be there when that happens to you!" I assured her that would never happen. I said, "I'm a participant not competing for the win. I'm only competing with myself."

My love for pushing myself was beginning to take over most of my free time. I bid a shift at work that would allow me to train daily and not interfere with family. Stacy and I always said life began at three o'clock when the yellow school bus stops in front of the house. Drake would swim daily. So, if there was a free lane in the pool, I would swim while he practiced. I would struggle like crazy with swimming. The young kids made it look effortless, but it was very difficult.

While trying to get efficient with swimming my friend, Jim, and I had started training for another half marathon. It's called the Urban Bourbon. Again, Louisville is known for horse racing and bourbon. This race went very well for both of us. At the finish line runners can sample local bourbons and beers. I don't know if it was because we just had a good race or the bourbon talking, but we decided to start training for a marathon.

Jim and I didn't know but we had a wonderful resource under our nose. A friend at work had completed marathons, ultra-marathons, and the Ironman! He immediately became my go to guy. I probably wore him out with all my questions. His first bit of advice was to get a training plan and stick with it. Jim and I found a plan that would download to our watches. I'm a fan of structure. I wanted to stick exactly to the plan. He just wanted to run. This plan consisted of three short to medium distance runs during the week and the long run on the weekend. The longest training run prior to the race was twenty miles. We had to start looking for routes that could accommodate these distances and keep us off busy streets. We got creative where we would run.

Sometimes we ran through some pretty sketchy areas of Louisville. During our training, we would go to the gym to weight train and swim for cross training. Very rarely did we take a day off.

Drake and I registered for a super sprint triathlon. It was early spring, so it was a winter format: bike, run then swim. Drake had to borrow my wife's mountain bike, and I was still riding an old borrowed 10 speed. Drake did very well. Of course, he excelled in the water, and I realized I had a huge hurdle to overcome if I would ever want to compete in an Ironman. As Jim and I continued to train for the marathon, we would comment on how amazing the body is. What used to be difficult is now basically a warmup.

As our mileage increased the need for nutrition on the run was coming into play. We asked a mutual friend from work what he used and started with that. We started using Goo. Imagine the consistency of toothpaste. That's what some of the supplements were like. Training your gut is just as important as the rest of your body. You need to make sure your gut can handle what you're feeding it. Having an upset stomach during a four-hour run is not fun.

The morning of our twenty-mile training run I picked up Jim and we drove to The Parklands in Louisville, Kentucky. One great thing about training with someone is it keeps you accountable. There were so many mornings I would have stayed in bed, but I knew Jim would be ready to go. I know he felt the same way too. We parked the car in a place where we thought the round-trip run would be twenty miles. When we got to the north end of the park, we knew we were going to have to continue beyond the car to get required distance. By the time we got back to the car I was done, mentally and physically exhausted. I think our distance was around eighteen miles. Jim, on the other hand, was ready to go. He kept saying, let's go twenty-two. Let's just run a full marathon. I finally said, "if I had a knife right now, I'd cut you!" We turned around and finished twenty. I learned how much mental strength it was going to take that morning for the race.

We are now in the tapering part of training. Basically, the hard part is over and you're healing your body for race day. It's another mental challenge because your body is used to long distances and now, you're only putting in very few miles. You must trust the plan. A few days prior to the race I was going nuts. I had a ton of energy and I was thinking I was losing strength from not putting the miles in. Jim and I started a new tradition by going out for wings and a couple beers the night before a race! I'm not sure how good of an idea this was, but we called it carb loading!

It's race day! I didn't get much sleep the night before. I worried if I brought everything: GPS watch, food, camelback for water, etc. We arrived at the start line with just minutes to spare. The gun sounded, and we're off! This is a combined half and full marathon race. About 20,000 runners are on the course. About 5,000 are full marathon runners. The first few miles everyone is running together. Somewhere around mile six orange cones start dividing the runners. Half marathoners on the left. Full marathoners on the right. This is when it started getting real. I had always been in the lane with all the people. That day, I was in the lane that was very empty. We kept telling ourselves, run your race, keep your heart rate in "the zone", and stay hydrated. There was a long way to go. As we ran through Indianapolis the course was supported well with people.

High school drum lines were out there. People playing music along the streets. Live bands performing in their front yards. Even college kids cheering us on as we ran through Butler University. Just prior to Butler a man had a table set up. His sign said, "water is overrated." His table was full of cups of beer! I was surprised how many people were taking him up on his offer. As the miles started adding up, fewer people were around. There was no more music, bands, and very few spectators. It was just you and your mind. We were told your race will begin at mile 20. Things will hurt that have never hurt before. You will see runners getting sick, cramping up, and quitting. If you just stick to your plan, you'll be okay. It was true. Jim and I kept moving forward and finished our first marathon!

We had all kinds of resources that we didn't know about. Another guy at work was training for Ironman Maryland. He became another asset and always had great advice. A father of one of Drakes teammates, Chad, was an Ironman too. I really started to lean on him for information. Chad was way out of my league but always willing to help. He suggested joining a multi-sport club named Louisville Landsharks. He was a member and said the club had group training. Open water swim sessions at Deam Lake were offered. I knew I was going to have to overcome that fear. There would be no lane lines and no wall to hang onto if I needed a break. My first open water swim was terrifying. I remember someone saying, "fish nibble, snakes bite!" Can I say I hate snakes! What was I thinking? The club would organize multiple distance bike rides after swimming. I would swim about 1/2 mile and ride the 25-mile bike route. The club was great! They had every level of athlete. No one was ever left behind. There was always someone willing to help if you needed anything. I continue to be a member today.

Dave during the bike portion of Ironman
Muncie.

The journey is a part of the process.

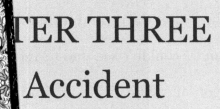

TER THREE

Accident

b, Jim and I were running two ticipated in an Olympic distance started to finalize my plan for Ironman Louisville. On July 6, 2016, I completed Ironman Muncie. It's a half distance Ironman triathlon - 1.2-mile swim, 56-mile bike and a half marathon (13.1 miles). Total distance is 70.3 miles. The swim was terrifying for me. Open water had people swimming over you with no visibility under water. You were constantly kicked, punched, and pushed out of the way. Within the first 100 yards, I remember having a panic attack. I looked up and was disoriented.

There was a buoy close, so I swam to it and got my bearings together. After the second turn, the sun was directly in your face and I couldn't see due to reflection from the water. I then got off course and swam into a pontoon boat. I had to orient myself again and swim the final leg. I kept telling myself to calm down and not give up - keep moving forward. At the transition between bike and run, I remember seeing my cheer team - my family. I was crying and worried about a pair of old shoes and Jim's shirt that was left behind.

The bike portion was long and windy. The wind made it hard to maintain my speed. The course description said it was flat, but it was rolling hills. I decided after that I would need to upgrade my bike before a full distance. Stacy thought I was crying from seeing them, but I was mentally gone at this point.

The run was difficult and added to my mental state. I kept reminding myself to run to the next mailbox. I had to overcome the voices in my head telling me to quit. One of the rules is no one can help you during the race. When I was insight of the finish line, my daughter, Morgan, saw me and started to run to greet me. I remember yelling at her and saying to stay back so I wouldn't get disqualified. When I crossed the finish line, I was incredibly happy, but knew I had a long way to go to complete a full distance Ironman in the coming year. Jim and I completed two more marathons over the next few months. One being a team relay with people from work. My portion was 6 miles. A very easy run for me. I started adding miles to build my endurance back.

On July 1, 2017 I met Harry, Jim, and Susan for a ride through the hills of southern Indiana. I had upgraded my bike to a triathlon bike, a pearl-white Cannondale Slice. I named her Pearl. She was full carbon fiber and so beautiful. She looked fast sitting still. We started at Harry and Susan's house in Floyds Knobs and they led us on the route. We planned on doing 30 miles that day. The hills were difficult but going downhill was a blast! We turned onto Chapel Hill Road that would take us back to their house. As we started to go down the hill my friend said, "last hill, make it count." We took off. I was second in line. At the bottom of the hill the road turned right and crossed a narrow bridge. A white SUV came in the opposite direction. I got on my brakes hard. The road was a little wet and my back tire started to come out from under me. I remember thinking this person is going to be mad because I'm going to sideswipe them. Well, that is what happened. My bike went on the right into the ditch, and my body hit the back quarter panel of the vehicle. It was $2,000 worth of damage to the car. Pearl was not damaged. She had only a few scratches and the chain was off. I on the other hand was damaged.

The next thing I see is the sunlight coming through the trees as I'm on the road. I hear people asking if I'm conscious. I said, "yes, I'm awake." They kept telling me not to move. I asked my friends how I was lying in the road because I couldn't feel my body. I could see blood running from my nose onto the pavement, and I could see my left hand. I tried to move my hand, but it wouldn't. While lying on the road my friends watched for oncoming traffic. It seemed like it took forever for the ambulance to arrive. After getting in the ambulance, they did a quick check on what I could feel. I couldn't feel or move anything below my shoulders. I had feeling in my shoulders, but they wouldn't move. The driver of the ambulance was new and didn't know his way around the knobs. I had to interrupt the paramedic who was arguing with the driver because I had blood running in my eyes. All I could think about was getting to the hospital.

My wife and daughter met us at the emergency room. Our son came from work shortly after. All I could say to her was, "I'm sorry". I was beginning to realize our future had just changed. We had so many things we wanted to do, just the two of us. As of then, those plans had to be put on hold. I do not remember much after this. Stacy said I would ask her and the kids to hold onto my shoulder or face because I couldn't feel anything lower. Everyone wanted to hold my hand, but it really didn't do me any good. The doctors ordered an MRI, and the results were not good! When the nurse brought me back up to emergency, she hit me in the nose while taking her gloves off. She felt horrible and it just added to the current pain. I never thought about paralysis. I thought I probably had a stinger and I'd be back to training in a couple weeks. After about 8 long hours in ER room #6, I was transferred to the ICU Trauma - 9th floor, East Wing.

The next few days were a blur. Stacy and the kids were worried, and Morgan called Stacy's sister to come down for extra support. Stacy needed her. She has always been like a second mother to her. There is twelve years difference between them and she's always there for her no matter what. Because the accident happened over a holiday weekend, I had to wait for surgery. My family didn't leave my side. They were able to watch the 4th of July fireworks from the penthouse waiting room of UofL Intensive Care Unit (ICU).

ICU was a crazy area as you can imagine. So busy, people coming and going at all hours. The floor was full of patients. Another male in the unit was in a motorcycle accident. Stacy said the doctors and nurses would get us confused. After being added to the schedule on July 5th, I had my surgery. The surgery took 5.5 hours. I went down to be prepped for surgery early. My surgery was the last to be completed that day. It was a long day for them. They waited patiently and tried to stay positive. This was hard since all the other families were leaving, and they were still waiting. Once the doctor was finished with the surgery, he spoke with the family. He said it went as well as could be and it would be a waiting game from here on out to see what movement would be regained.

I broke my neck, back, and nose in the accident. The worst break was my neck. I broke my cervical spine in the C3

(Cervical 3) area which is located just under the brain stem and my T5 (Thoracic 5) - mid back area *(See photo on next page)*. The C3 break damaged my spinal cord at that location. I was fused from C2-C6. It is still hard to believe I have a rod and lots of screws holding my body together. This injury left me paralyzed from the neck down.

Image on next page is from https://www.christopherreeve.org website.

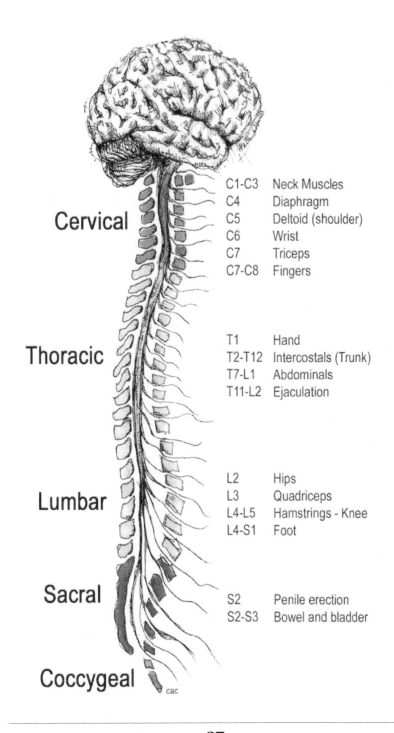

C1-C3	Neck Muscles
C4	Diaphragm
C5	Deltoid (shoulder)
C6	Wrist
C7	Triceps
C7-C8	Fingers

T1	Hand
T2-T12	Intercostals (Trunk)
T7-L1	Abdominals
T11-L2	Ejaculation

L2	Hips
L3	Quadriceps
L4-L5	Hamstrings - Knee
L4-S1	Foot

S2	Penile erection
S2-S3	Bowel and bladder

I want to emphasize to always wear a bike helmet. Stacy always wondered why I got such an expensive helmet. Well, IT SAVED MY LIFE! It was severely damaged. Drake wanted to get a new helmet for me since the company would replace it. This never happened because I wanted to keep it. Later, I called the CEO of the helmet company. He asked me to send him photos of the helmet. He said after seeing it, "You hit hard!" He said the impact was between 200 and 250 Linear G Forces. I had no idea what that meant so I Googled it. Below is a graph of what I found. As I looked it over, I am very lucky to be alive. As you can see my accident exceeded a fatal bicycle accident with a helmet.

a (g)	Acceleration and the Human Body
	event
2.9	sneeze
3.5	cough
3.6	crowd jostle
4.1	slap on back
8.1	hop off step
10.1	plop down in chair
60	chest acceleration limit during car crash at 48 km/h with airbag
70 - 100	crash that killed Diana, Princess of Wales, 1997
150 - 200	head acceleration limit during bicycle crash with helmet
	Source: Spine, June 1994

Luckily, I was not on a ventilator. Most injuries that high on the spinal cord require a ventilator because the diaphragm is paralyzed and can leave you in a vegetated state. I had a neck brace on to protect my neck. All I could do was lay in bed and stare at the ceiling but without my glasses everything was blurry. This added to my confusion and fear of the unknown. I was also on a lot of pain medicine. It was great for resting but made me have crazy dreams and paranoia. Stacy never left my side in case my fear returned, and she didn't want me to be alone.

I had so many visitors, sometimes a line down the hall. They would bring gifts, food, and magazines. We shared them with all the staff in the unit. Because of the confusion between the motorcycle accident and myself, the nurses would send our friends to the wrong person. It's funny now, but I was even told a friend had a full conversation with the guy finally realizing the mistake. His head was bandaged up so that made it difficult to tell. Our church family would visit twice a week. One visitor stands out the most. She was from the prayer team. As she began to pray with me, I felt something leave my body. It was like a huge weight leaving me. I knew that was God telling me I was going to be okay. I don't know how I'll end up, but God is letting me know I'll be okay. My faith that was instilled in me was also going to be tested. I always heard God doesn't give us more than we can handle. I told myself this is a lot, but let's go! After several days, I was able to wiggle my toes on my left foot. Everyone was so excited and thanking God! This was very encouraging. We continued anticipating what movement would be next. Everyone continued to pray, and God answered those prayers.

I was labelled as a C-3, incomplete quadriplegic (quad). We didn't know what it meant. Remember C3 is Cervical 3 on the spine and incomplete meaning has some feeling below the injury level. A quadriplegic has no movement from the chest down whereas, a paraplegic has use of their arms.

From the Paralysis Reference Guide, Spinal cord injury (SCI) involves damage to the nerves within the bony protection of the spinal canal. The most common cause of cord injury is trauma, although damage can occur from various diseases acquired at birth or later in life, from tumors, electric shock, poisoning or loss of oxygen related to surgical or underwater mishaps. The spinal cord does not have to be severed for a loss of function to occur. In fact, in most people with SCI, the spinal cord is bruised and intact. Since the spinal cord coordinates body movement and sensation, an injured cord loses the ability to send and receive messages from the brain to the body's systems that control sensory, motor, and autonomic function below the level of injury; this often results in paralysis. *(From Christopher and Dana Reeve Foundation - Paralysis Reference Guide, pg. 33.)*

While there's almost always hope of recovering some function after a spinal cord injury, it is generally true that people with incomplete injuries have a better chance of getting more return. The sooner muscles start working again, the better the chances are of additional recovery. When muscles come back later, after the first several weeks, they are more likely to be in the arms than in the legs. If there is some improvement and additional muscles recover function, the chances are better that more improvement is possible. The longer there is no improvement, the lower the odds it will start to happen on its own. The spinal cord is organized into segments along its length, noted by their position along the thirty-three vertebrae of the backbone. Nerves from each segment are responsible for motor and sensory functions for specific regions of the body (if you map this, it's called a dermatome, right). In general, the higher in the spinal column an injury occurs, the more function a person will lose. The segments in the neck, or cervical region, referred to as C1 through C8, control signals to the neck, arms, hands, and, in some cases, the diaphragm.

Injuries to this area result in tetraplegia, or as it is more commonly called, quadriplegia.

Injury above the C3 level may require a ventilator for the person to breathe. Injury above the C4 level usually means loss of movement and sensation in all four limbs, although often shoulder and neck movement is available to facilitate sip-and-puff devices for mobility, environmental control, and communication. C5 injuries often spare the control of shoulder and biceps, but there is not much control at the wrist or hand. Those at C5 can usually feed themselves and independently handle many activities of daily living. C6 injuries generally allow wrist control, enough to be able to drive adaptive vehicles and handle personal hygiene, but those affected at this level often lack fine hand function. Individuals with C7 and T1 injuries can straighten their arms and can typically handle most self-care activities, though they still may have dexterity problems with hands and fingers.

Nerves in the thoracic, or upper back region (T1 through T12), relay signals to the torso and some parts of the arms. Injuries from T1 to T8 usually affect control of the upper torso, limiting trunk movement as the result of a lack of abdominal muscle control. Lower thoracic injuries (T9 to T12) allow good trunk control and good abdominal muscle control. Those injured in the lumbar, or mid-back region just below the ribs (L1 through L5), can control signals to the hips and legs. A person with an L4 injury can often extend the knees. The sacral segments (S1 through S5) lie just below the lumbar segments in the mid-back and control signals to the groin, toes, and some parts of the legs. *(pgs. 35-37)*

I spent a total of twelve days in ICU. My doctors and nurses were becoming like family to me. They helped save my life! Word spread quick of my accident. I was known as the 2nd Southern Indiana tragic or near fatal accident from a bicycle. To continue my rehab, I was going to be moved to another facility to start my recovery. We were referred to UofL's Frazier Rehab Institute just down the street. We had no idea what was happening; just rolling with the punches. My family made an appointment to meet with the admission's director at Frazier. She of course had a family member who was in the Louisville Landsharks club, so she was familiar with the sport. I had no idea the rehab hospital I was going to, is one of the best in the country for spinal cord injury.

On moving day, it was quite an experience. I was moved to a shared room for a few hours waiting for my transfer. The person who was with me had just been release from prison. He was on the phone most of the time arguing with his significant other and was so loud we heard his whole life history. He also would pull his IV out to get attention from the nurses. The ambulance ride took so long. Stacy could have pushed me down the road quicker. Despite the delays we knew we had to keep moving forward.

Reference: Christopher and Dana Reeve Foundation - Paralysis Reference Guide

Stacy and Dave keeping busy and learning their
new normal in life.

**We daily adjust to the hand we have been
dealt with heart and the goal to win.**

Keep Moving Forward!

CHAPTER FOUR
The Recovery Zone

After arriving at Frazier, we were greeted by wonderful staff. The place was amazingly big and nice. Everyone was so positive. We instantly felt like home. We didn't know at that time we would live here for 65 days. My room, #1006, was located on the spinal cord injury floor. I had an extra bed so Stacy or the kids would stay with me. Night-time was absolutely frightening for me. My mind would go crazy at night. Being unable to move was terrifying. It made me feel so claustrophobic and trapped. I would wake whoever was staying with me and ask them to just talk to me. I tried to listen to soothing music and podcasts. They didn't help. My mental strength was put to the test nightly. I never knew what anxiety was. It was all new to me. The panic attacks happened regularly. I would feel lightheaded, have heart palpitations, and feel nauseous. Stacy was aware of the signs of a panic attack and helped me understand how to deal with it.

Everyday started with me being dressed and hoisted out of bed with a Hoyer lift. A Hoyer lift is basically a harness that I was wrapped in and strapped to a lift system in the ceiling. It would lift me out of bed and into my power wheelchair. My occupational therapists would help me relearn how to brush my teeth and wash my face. One of the worst things about being a quad is not being able to control your bowel and bladder. Every four to six hours my bladder had to be drained. This was either done by Stacy or the nurses. Stacy was such a pro. In the evening I was lifted by a Hoyer to the bedside commode for my "bowel program." This procedure would take about an hour and was very stressful.

I started receiving physical and occupational therapy the next day. Not only was it physically exhausting but also mentally. At first the therapists would come to my room twice a day. Physical therapy was only once a day. It was so frustrating, my brain would tell my body to move, but my body was not responding. I had to retrain my body to do everything, even the simplest things. I started to realize this was going to be the toughest training plan I've ever had. With this training plan you never have an off day or a cheat day. If I wanted to gain some sort of a normal life this was going to take everything I had. Stacy and I had plans, and I owed it to her to train like I've never trained before.

After a week I was moved to the inpatient gym for my sessions. It had floor to ceiling windows. I remember the first time looking out and seeing the words "Never Give Up" painted on the wall below across the street. This was a great motivator to keep going. They had me standing and weight baring almost immediately. We would go to the gym and work on other daily activities that I had to retrain my body to do. Each session was about an hour long. In the beginning it was so frustrating because my hands were not responding well. I would have to try and pick up pegs and put them in a pegboard. They had me doing puzzles, squeezing objects, and reaching for things just to get my fingers to wake up. My therapists learned quickly that I wasn't afraid of hard work. They weren't afraid to push me to exhaustion.

My physical therapist, while being held by a harness, would be on the floor moving my legs and feet. She was retraining my legs to move. She would keep telling me "move your legs, David!" Physical therapy was also an hour session. Then I had a short break to eat my lunch. I would try to feed myself, but I remember not being able to hold the utensils. The nurses would assist me as well as friends who visited. To be honest the hospital food wasn't too bad. I was never alone. Stacy had to work so she put together a daily schedule for friends to come. I would have a few minutes to rest. Most people would stay and go to therapy with me which was very thoughtful. I would have occupational and physical therapy after lunch. My spine doctor and his team would stop by my room regularly. Every Tuesday they would meet to go over my results and decide if my game plan needed to be changed. The doctor discussed with us about the outpatient spinal cord gym that was one floor up from the inpatient floor. He said he was trying to get me a spot on one of their treadmills. The thought of that was exciting and very frightening.

The equipment in the 11th floor gym was paid for by the Christopher Reeve Foundation. At that time only a few rehabilitation hospitals were equipped by them. I was so fortunate to be from New Albany, Indiana and only cross the bridge to Louisville, Kentucky to be there. Some people travel from all over the country and must move here for their services. I was put in a device that reminded me of something like a parachute harness. It was also suspended from the ceiling. It would keep me balanced as I stood. I was put on a waiting list for the use of the equipment.

Motivated mouse: epidural stimulation plus treadmill training equals function. (Photo from Gregoire Courtine Lab) pg. 39

Reeve used treadmill training, a type of physical therapy that forces the legs to move in a pattern of walking as the body is suspended in a harness above a moving treadmill. The theory is that the spinal cord can interpret incoming sensory signals; the cord itself is smart. It can carry out movement commands without brain input. Locomotion is managed by a system called a central pattern generator (CPG), which activates the pattern of stepping. Stepping during treadmill training sends sensory information to the CPG, reminding the spinal cord how to step.

Scientists describe the reactivation due to stepping as plasticity—the nervous system is not "hard wired" and appears to have the ability to adapt itself to new stimulation. Researchers are learning much more about the CPG and how to activate it. Rehabilitation techniques have evolved to the point that exercise and physical activity are an essential component of recovery. For the person with a spinal cord injury, it's best to stay active and always strive for the maximum outcome (page 43).

After a couple of weeks, I was granted a spot on the treadmill in the gym. I was scared to death! I had no idea what I was getting myself in to. I had lost a lot of strength and weight. I was weak at this point. I weighed 200 pounds the day of my accident. They weighed me that day and I was down to 148 pounds. The first person to approach me in the gym was probably mid-twenties, extremely fit, and intimidated the heck out of me. He harnessed me up to an attachment from the ceiling and got me ready for a treadmill session. I quickly learned inpatient therapy was difficult and outpatient is just as hard. The harness would allow me to bear a certain percentage of my body weight on my legs. I couldn't feel my legs or feet but there was a mirror in front of me so I could see what was happening.

On the treadmill, I had a physical therapist and three technicians helping me. One person would guide my hips. Another person would step my right leg and another on my left. The fourth person ran the computer which monitored the time, speed, and body weight percentage. They would rotate positions because moving paralyzed legs is no easy task. I now understand why they're in great shape. Every person in this gym is fit. The therapists and technicians are all young but exceptionally good at what they do. I would come to this gym once or twice weekly if a slot was available.

I would also walk the stairs. This was so draining. Sometimes my blood pressure would drop, and I would collapse which isn't good on stairs.

During my days at Frazier, Stacy and I were interviewed by Extol Magazine and WHAS11 (a local magazine and tv station). They both had heard about my story and wanted an interview. We were even on a billboard from what we were told. When WHAS11 came for the interview, my therapist had me show off my walking skills. An impatient friend was teasing me and asked if I wanted to race. Well, he won, but I continued to be determined to work on going faster.

After two and half months of inpatient rehab, it was time to go home! Stacy and I were excited but also scared to death. What the heck do we do now? I'm basically a 48-year-old infant, totally dependent on someone else. New Albany's Prosser Career Education Centers Building Trades class (Stacy's employer) had built a ramp in our garage. They even installed a wider door so I could get in the house. This made us both so thrilled to be able to be under cover and out of the elements to get in and out of the house. We converted our dining room into my hospital room. We had a hospital bed and a portable Hoyer lift in there as well as other hospital equipment. Stacy had to learn how to put me in the Hoyer sling. She'd then hoist me up and swing me around into my wheelchair or into the bathroom. Bathroom routines and showers were and still are very challenging. Our bathroom had to be renovated to accommodate my needs. The jacuzzi tub and shower were removed and an accessible shower was built. Stacy is my rock! Most caretakers abandon the patient due to the stress and not being able to handle the day-to-day routine.

Skin breakdown is something that I must watch. Pressure sores are quite common with a spinal cord injury. We always need to be aware of a condition called autonomic dysreflexia (AD). This can be fatal if not stopped quickly. Since I don't have feeling over most of my body, AD can start if something is bothering me. It can be caused by several things. Something as small as a hang nail. This condition was probably one of our biggest fears about leaving the hospital.

Here is another explanation of AD from the ChristopherReeve.org website:

What is autonomic dysreflexia?

Autonomic dysreflexia (AD) is a potentially life-threatening medical emergency that affects people with spinal cord injuries at the T6 level or higher. Although rare, some people with T7 and T8 injuries can develop AD. For most people, AD can be easily treated as well as prevented. The key is knowing your baseline blood pressure, triggers, and symptoms.

When triggered, AD requires quick and correct action or there may be serious consequence such as a stroke. Because many health professionals are not familiar with this condition, it is important for people who are at risk for AD, including the people close to them, to recognize the symptoms and know how to act.

It's important for at-risk individuals to know their baseline blood pressure values and to communicate to healthcare providers how to identify as well as manage an AD emergency.

Some of the signs of AD include high blood pressure, pounding headache, flushed face, sweating above the level of injury, goose flesh below the level of injury, nasal stuffiness, nausea, and a slow pulse (slower than 60 beats per minute). Symptoms will vary based on the individual.

Causes of AD

Autonomic dysreflexia is caused by an irritant below the level of injury, including:

Bladder: irritation of the bladder wall, urinary tract infection, blocked catheter, or overfilled collection bag.

- Bowel: distended or irritated bowel, constipation or impaction, hemorrhoids, or anal infections.

- Other causes include skin infection or irritation, cuts, bruises, abrasions, or pressure sores (decubitus ulcers), ingrown toenails, burns (including sunburn and burns from hot water) and tight or restrictive clothing.

In September after a week at home, I started outpatient therapy at Frazier. This was going to be tough. Three to five hours of therapy at least three or four days per week. Stacy had to keep working so I would be riding public transportation out of Louisville. For the first few months, I had someone riding with me. The hospital is about ten miles from home but some days it would take 90 minutes back and forth. It's a shared ride. This bus system is only available for disabled people. We are picked up and dropped off wherever we need to go. It's a wonderful service. You must be screened by the company and then make reservations a week prior.

The bus can arrive 15 minutes prior to your pickup time and 15 minutes after pickup time to return home. This gives them a half hour window. So, you know what the time frame will be. If you must change your pickup return time due to an appointment running late the Transit Authority of River City (TARC) will put you on a will call pickup which normally takes up to 90 minutes. I also have some great stories! I had a driver that was afraid to cross the bridges and prayed outload to Jesus to get her safely over to the other side. Eventually, I would be on my own. Nothing ever happens when you're with someone, only when I'm by myself. Once, the bus broke down and we had to be transferred to another bus in the middle of the street. We hit a tree one morning and had to wait for the supervisor to arrive and determine if we could continue. I have witnessed numerous fights and even drug deals in the street in broad daylight! Mostly I have met some amazing people from drivers to passengers. They have become like family too.

Normally my therapy was scheduled first thing in the morning. Physical therapy would wear me out. The treadmill would cause me to have spastic muscles. When the staff working with my legs started to sweat, I knew they were working hard. After the treadmill we would work on what was called over ground. Learning to stand from a sitting position was and still is one of the hardest things to do. I still struggle getting out of a seat when my legs are at a 90-degree angle. We would also work on balance and endurance when I was able to stand on my own. Friends would come over to Frazier and help feed me lunch. After lunch I would start occupational therapy. My therapist and advocate would hook me up to electrical stimulation. This was like a TENS Unit on steroids. The stimulation shocked my muscles into working. It also strengthened my muscles. The staff always made it fun and bearable! They would always get me caught up on reality tv as well as other current trends. Because of the floor to ceiling windows, I would quiz them on airplanes approaching the Louisville Airport. After a few months they could tell me what type of airplane was landing. I'm an aviation nerd and it showed up there.

Every few weeks the therapist would have to complete an evaluation of my progress. I always told them I don't test well. My advocate ended up telling the therapists to spring the evaluation on me, so I didn't have time to stress about it. The more I stressed, the tighter my muscles became. The physical therapy evaluation would take around an hour consisting of everything we worked on daily. Again, sit to stands from a low chair always played tricks on me. We would walk in the hallway. A ten-meter fast walk was always on the list and a continuous six-minute walk was performed to measure endurance. Occupational therapy was not as physical but just as stressful. Range of motion, trying to sit up using only your ab muscles and using small objects to work my fine motor skills were part of their test.

I was in and out of the hospital several times due to UTI's which are common with foley catheters. The crazy thing is once the EMTs or hospital staff learned I was a quadriplegic they would panic. They wanted to transfer me to UofL Hospital in Kentucky. One time I asked for a walker and the nurses were hesitant to get me one. All I wanted to do was get some exercise and get out of bed for a change of routine.

As I was working on getting stronger, Stacy was in a constant battle with bills, insurance, Social Security, and maintaining things around the house. I am truly blessed to have her by my side. She basically works two full time jobs. One of her jobs is an administrative assistant and the other one is taking care of me. We could get no help through our insurance. Just keeping the schedule up to date with all my doctor appointments was crazy. Between my neurologist, urologist, physiatrist, and therapists, my schedule was very full. At first, I would have at least one doctor appointment a week.

That fall, our neighbor asked if she could have a fundraiser for us. The bills were crazy and overwhelming as you can imagine. The event was a tremendous success, and it was a night we'll remember forever. I think we had over 500 people there that night. One coming all the way from Texas. I was able to get up out of wheelchair and take a few steps with help. This was the first time I did this in public without my extra therapy family around. I don't think there was a dry eye in the place. Everyone cheered! The Louisville Landsharks had a fundraiser also for us. Morgan and Stacy represented me at their event. We were able to pay bills, get a manual wheelchair, and remodel our bathroom with the money raised. To add to the fundraising, Stacy and the kids sold t-shirts and bracelets that said Dave Will Ride Again and Helmets Save Lives. They were Kelly green in color for spinal cord injury awareness. It was great getting photos of friends and family all over the world wearing them and showing their support. People really came together in a time of need.

Another obstacle we were trying to overcome was not being "trapped" at home. My power chair is wonderful but it's huge and heavy weighing over 450 lbs. We had a small SUV, and we didn't want to make the jump to an accessible van. They are awfully expensive, and I felt confident that I wasn't going to be in that big chair forever. After trying a hitch mounted rack, we decided to buy a small trailer. Stacy now had to learn to pull a trailer with my chair on it. We started going to high school basketball games. They are fun and great way to get out of the house for a couple hours. But one hurdle she dealt with was the weather (normally cold or rainy). It all took time. She would have to get me situated in the car, drive the wheelchair up the ramp, and then try to strap it securely to the trailer.

I continued to improve in therapy, but my spasticity was starting to limit my progress. Spasticity feels like a constant charlie horse that won't go away. I have this all throughout my body. Sometimes it takes everything Stacy has to bend my legs to get me in the car. If I sneeze or something scares me my spasms kick in. Watch out if you are in front of me, you might get kicked!

My physiatrist started talking about a pump that would be implanted in my body and deliver medicine directly to my spinal cord. As the spasticity increased, I decided to have a test done to see if a pump would make a difference. This was an outpatient procedure. The pain management doctor inserted a needle into my spinal cord with a test dose. Within hours my legs were not nearly as tight, and walking was easier. I decided right then I wanted the surgery. The thought of having something the size of a hockey puck in my lower abdomen was weird but if it helped, I wanted to take the chance. One downfall was the pump would help my legs but not my arms or hands. I would still have to take medicine to keep them loose. I had the surgery in August 2018. As of now, the pump gets refilled about every six weeks by my physiatrist, and the battery should last about five years. At that time, I will have to have a new one implanted. I still have spasticity, but it is greatly reduced.

Outpatient therapy continued three to four days per week. My walking and balance were getting much better. My arms and hands were still not responding as well as I hoped. I was getting new braces to wear weekly. I started getting Botox injections in my arms and hands. Botox basically puts muscles to sleep so others can get stronger. Stacy always wanted to go to the appointments just in case they had extra! I asked how many units of Botox were used for a normal procedure, i.e., forehead injections. The doctor said, "about 50". I asked how many units am I getting? He said, "700!

Even with the help of Botox, my hands started to close like fists. I was referred to a hand surgeon to see what he thought could be done. When I first met him, I was scared to death. As you can tell I have lots of doctors and until then, they had either been my age or younger. This guy could be my grandpa!

I learned very quickly to not judge a book by its cover. This surgeon is well known locally as well as around the world for what he has done. He has two hospitals in Korea named after him. Turns out, he is one of my favorite doctors to go see. Always thinking of ways to help me. He makes sure Stacy is okay too. He recommended tendon lengthening surgery for my right hand. The preferred outcome was to release my fingers so my hands would move more freely. In November of 2018, I had surgery on my right arm.

A year later in October, I had double hand surgery. The same surgeon completed on my right-hand muscle transfers in wrist, fused a joint in my thumb, and released tendons on the top of hand. On the left-hand, tendons were lengthened for my fingers. I was back at Frazier for inpatient therapy right after the procedure. My therapist knew me from when I was inpatient two years before. She knew exactly how to motivate me and kept me on my toes. I was quickly reminded of how exhausting putting puzzles together could be. I was also doing physical therapy while inpatient. I had the same physical therapist again and we picked right up like we never stopped. I had many staff from my past stay stopped by my room and I remembered how great these people were. They helped me during the tough times. I remember the staff was concerned because I was different this time around. They couldn't understand why I was acting differently. I told them the last time I was inpatient; I couldn't feel the pain my body was going through this time was different and very painful. I never liked taking pain killers and the doctors reminded me I had to stay ahead of the pain to recover. I was released from Frazier after two weeks to head back home. I remember telling Stacy that they are our second family, our Frazier family.

In early 2019, I started working with vocational rehab. This organization helps people with disabilities get back to work. We met with my management team at work for a site evaluation. The equipment needed for me to return to work was minimal. It was great to know that returning to my job was possible if I passed the training. The equipment I used at home to practice was purchased by Easter Seals. I still was not physically ready to give my notice to return. I wanted to continue my recovery knowing improvement may slow down. Statistics show that after three years improvement diminishes. I wanted to take full advantage of my time because once back to work my therapy may only be one day per week. I turned in my return-to-work letter October of 2020. In January of 2021, I was able to have a trial run with my job. I was able to do flight plans as I did four years ago. I might be a quad, but God made sure I kept my brain.

Reference: Christopher and Dana Reeve Foundation - Paralysis Reference Guide

Dave's training day back at work. He has done this job
over 25 years and did it without missing a beat!

IRONCLAD FAMILY

The Unbreakable Strength to Keep Moving Forward

CHAPTER FIVE
Ironclad Wife

Stacy Miller:

One thing about Dave and me, we moved away from our family at an early age, so Dave could continue his career. He always wanted to be an air traffic controller, but things fell through. He was not called for an interview because it was soon after the air traffic control strike and they weren't hiring at the time. So, the next best thing would be to become a flight dispatcher for a major airline. Dave got a job in Indianapolis back in 1992 with American Trans Air (a charter airline), so I moved with him. Growing up in a very small town, I was extremely excited to start our new journey in Indy. It was full of life and lots of fun things to do. With my job, we were able to go to go to car races, Pacer and Colts games, and Dave and I would go to concerts monthly. We became very independent, wild, and free at the age of 22. It was tough, but we managed. Dave worked two jobs so we could pay our bills.

I always wanted to be closer to our family but with his line of work you had to go to the job wherever it was. I remember getting a call from him saying, "you ready for this? I got an interview with UPS in Louisville." It was a dream of Dave's to work for UPS. I loved Indy, but how could I keep him from a dream job. So, a few months later we were living in Louisville. Twenty-Five years later we are living in New Albany, Indiana and with 2 children (Morgan-21 & Drake-19), a beautiful house. We were living the life.

July 1, 2017 - It was a regular Saturday morning; Dave had been up early about 6:00 AM to start his normal training. He had been a dedicated triathlete since our kids were born. Always up early on the weekends to get his runs, biking, or swims in before his family would be up to start their day. It had rained the night before, so the roads were still a little wet which caused a delay in his routine of running and biking. I remember he was texting his friends asking if they thought the road were dry yet. He loved exercising. It was a great release for him after working third shift as a flight controller. I never stepped in his way. I never stated my concern or fear of him getting injured. I knew it was an important piece in the puzzle of life for him. It was a way for him to clear his mind.

I was getting my day started with our daughter Morgan at home. Drake was already at work. Morgan and I were hanging out catching up on tv shows we missed during the week. At about 11:25 AM, I received a phone call from Susan who was biking with Dave. I answered not even concerned. She told me Dave had been in a bicycle accident and he hit his head. Susan said he was going to the hospital via ambulance to be checked out, and she would come pick us up and take us there. Upon our arrival, we went straight to University of Louisville's Emergency Room. I was shocked to see him lying on the gurney strapped down and in a neck brace. He looked ok except for his face, which was bloody, and his nose was broken. He was very calm. I'm not sure if I was in shock or what, but I was thinking ok he's going to get bandaged up and we will be on our way. Never in a million years did I believe he was paralyzed from the neck down.

Everything was fast paced even though it took over 8 hours to get a room. The nurses and many doctors would come in and out taking him for x-rays, cat scans, MRI's etc. I never thought his injury was as bad as it was. Not Dave, he had been doing this for years and he was a pro. Dave was moved up to the ICU Trauma floor – 9 East. He was hooked up to so many machines. I had never felt so all alone. I had my kids, but I think I was in shock to realize what was happening. So, the kids got ahold of my sister and she was able to come down and be my support. I can't really tell you much about this time in the trauma unit. It is still very foggy to me.

I remember Dave was on so much pain medication, he was in and out of sleep having crazy dreams. He woke up at one time telling me he had to set up a meeting with the Attorney General, Jeff Sessions. Always trying to put a smile on our face even in this critical time. Not once do I remember the doctors saying he could die. Maybe I blocked it out. I don't know. Since his accident was over the fourth of July holiday, he had to wait a couple days to have surgery to repair his spine. I was by his side while he was in ICU. I do remember that terrible chair where I tried to sleep. On day eight, Dave was able to move his left toe. We were so excited! He will get better...he will! I remember reassuring myself. As the days drew on, I had to start thinking about what was best for Dave.

Our family visited Frazier Rehab and was asked if we would sign a contract for services at their facilities. After 14 days in the ICU, he was moved to Frazier on the 10th floor. It was a floor for spinal cord injuries. I remember the staff treating us like we were entering Disney World. I was even brought a bed so I could rest while there. They truly were amazing! Between my kids and I, we would stay every night with him. This lasted for 65 days. We had to set up a schedule based on our work schedules. Our days consisted of getting up at the hospital bright an early, showering there, off to work, back to hospital to sleep and start all over. The kids were unbelievable! It was trying times for all of us, but they were so mature and strong during this crazy time. I was so proud of them! Their lives were changing right in front of them. They took it so maturely. Not many 21 and 19-year-olds would do what these kids did. I knew at this point Dave and I did good at raising great kids. Putting others before themselves.

As Dave remained in rehab, I had to continue with our "normal" life changes. Morgan left for her junior year of college 3.5 hours away, and I moved my 19-year-old into his first year of college at ISU in Terre Haute. I had no idea what I was doing just living day by day. I was in the process of starting a new job. I was able to rearrange my work schedule to be with Dave. It was just so crazy. We had so many friends supporting us with prayers, food, gifts, and visiting us in the hospital daily. I even had a couple men spend the night with him just so I could have a break. I'm not sure where I would be today without them. As the kids left, I was starting to panic. How was I going to do this? I'm not a caregiver, maintenance man, or chef. I was freaking out inside but had to remain strong for Dave.

Days went by and his therapy was getting tougher. He was scheduled all day long, 5 to 6 days a week. He was still unable to do much independently. I remember having to go through the 24-nursing test. I had to be the caregiver, and the nurses critiqued everything I did. I was not ready but didn't have a choice. Insurance was pushing us out. It was time for me to take over. I have never been the "ah you poor baby, what can momma do," kind of person. Earlier when the kids were sick, I made them sleep on the bathroom floor so they would be close to the toilet. I would tell them it's much easier to clean up vomit on tile than in carpet. I was just not good at taking care of sick people, including my kids. Thank goodness, they were not sick too often.

On August 30, we were discharged. It was my time to shine as a caregiver. What was I going to do? How was I going to manage? These thoughts kept repeating in my head. I would go to bed tired...wake up exhausted. I was working eight-hour days and taking care of Dave the other 16. I had to come up with a schedule for Dave to get back and forth from Frazier, and get friends lined up to help take care of him while I worked. People helped where and when they could.

So, after almost 4 years, my feelings are still raw. I still get angry, have feel sorry for myself days, and days where I'm glad it is another day of living. It is a daily roller coaster. I realized you must live in the now. God never promises tomorrow. We are still trying to figure this whole thing out. It is a new challenge every day. We will be married 28 years, May 2021. We planned on renewing our vows, traveling, and just doing what we wanted to do as empty nesters. We were always very lively, adventurous people. We have a new way of life now. This is not the plan we had, but God won't give you more than you can handle and that is what we are doing one day at a time. God is Good!

Dave and Stacy celebrating their 26th anniversary.

I can conquer the world with one hand if you are holding the other.

Keep Moving Forward!

CHAPTER SIX
Team Miller

Morgan Miller:

It was spring, and I had finally made it to the place I had been thinking about for months. In a small room, pretty much a closet, I set in a computer desk chair across from a bearded man who would become the holder of all my secrets. He said, "have you ever talked to someone in this environment before?" I shook my head no, but said I know this was what I needed to do to better myself. There I sat in a seven by six room with a man I had never met before, and he asked me one question. "Why are you here?" Then it seemed like a landslide.

It was July 1st, 2017, I was home for summer break to make

some money before I go back to college in August. It was a Saturday, which was one of my favorite days growing up. Usually, when waking up, I would hear the lawnmower going. We would have a veggie plate for lunch, have a fast-food dinner, and spend the rest watching football—the perfect day. But on this day, I woke up, and there was no lawnmower. I went downstairs to accompany my mom on the couch and ask where my dad was. She told me he was training and should be home in thirty minutes. We sat and waited, probably going back and forth about celebrity gossip or plans for the day.

We got the call. It was from a family friend who was training with my dad that morning. She told my mom that she would be at our house to pick us up and take us to the hospital. She never told us how my dad was hurt, and I remember laughing with my mom on the porch about how he must have broken his leg or arm. This would be something that would happen to him since our family is full of klutzes. We get to the hospital and wait for a while in the waiting room. We finally see my dad. Blood, broken nose, neck brace, and he was strapped down on the bed. And the only first thing to come out of his mouth, "I'm so sorry." He knew. He knew that this was going to be the hardest thing we all had ever been through. After weeks of pain, tears, and sleepless nights, dad got to a stable place, Frazier Rehab. He finally smiled the smile that we hadn't seen in months—his purpose changed to making himself the better version of himself.

Mom, my brother, and I stayed strong for him. We stayed up late with him at the hospital, fed him, and found ways to make him happy when his memories of the accident creeped in. We continued to work; we pushed through like my dad used to push through for us: the anchor, the rock, the backbone to our family. The summer ends, and we all went our separate ways. My brother started his first year of college, my mom transitioned into becoming a nurse for my dad as well as a new job, and I went back to college to begin my junior year.

I was happy to leave. I wanted to forget about the summer, the pain, and the accident. That is precisely what I did until it all hit me in the face. My junior year was a struggle; my grades weren't the best, I picked up nasty habits, and my relationships were negatively affected. I remember getting angry fast and sad, even faster. My poor roommate, the sweetest soul, who had lost her mom a year prior, would be so forgiving of my behavior to her. She seemed to know what was making me like this. Finally, after I had opened my eyes, I concluded that it was time for me to see someone and talk.

After a few weeks of mustering up the courage, I made my way to fill out the paperwork to meet with a counselor. That next week, I found myself in a small room, nervous. Not knowing what was going to happen. He asks me, "so, why are you here?" I start crying and replied back, "I feel lost. I am not myself." I spent every Tuesday for the next three months in that computer chair. I told him about the accident, my relationships, and I cried, the most I have ever cried. He tells me I have been struggling with my mental health my whole life. Anxiety and depression seem like factors that are frequent in the stories that I had shared with him. Then he says something that I will never forget, "You are mourning; you have lost your dad."

On July 1st, I had lost my dad, my best friend, my counselor, and my protector. My mind was blown, and it finally made sense. I needed to grieve. I needed to find reassurance in the fact that the man who I had danced with all my life might not dance again. Dad was still dad. My bearded counselor started to give me homework, to write down every feeling I felt. To write lists of things that made me feel sad, mad, happy, and all the emotions in between.

Here is a note I wrote a week before I left college after my junior year to go home for the summer - "I am sad today; I miss my dad. I dreamt of him last night standing next to me. I miss his hugs. I miss seeing him mow. I miss driving with him. I miss seeing him dance in the kitchen. I miss seeing him in those blue shorts and a white t-shirt on the couch on his iPad. I can't wait to see him next week." Two years after counseling and I still cry, and I get mad at the fact that my dad had to go through something this terrible—the man who gave to others before himself is now paralyzed. I am thankful for whatever power that rules over our world that my dad is still here with us. His journey has just started, and I know it will end in his favor. My dad is strong. He will get this job done!

Drake Miller:

The morning of July 1st, 2017 was just like any other Saturday morning. Dad and I would usually leave the house at the same time, which was for training and/or work. That morning I was on my way to work at Enterprise, and I took a quick glance at my dad and asked the usual question, "how many?" He confidently responded back with an "only 26 miles." I did my usual sarcastic chuckle back and said, "ha-ha yeah, only 26" and confidently went on my way not knowing what was ahead of me.

It was never a surprise to get a text from my sister, but when I did it was something usually very important. Looking down at the text reading "hey, dad got in an accident, we're heading to the hospital," wasn't anything unsettling to me. I almost went on with my day thinking this was something we would laugh about at family dinner that night but knowing that Morgan texted me I knew it was serious. I decided to make my way over to the UofL Emergency Room. I knew in the back of my head it was something serious, but I still tried to find some joy in the situation to make everyone laugh.

Growing up I was a competitive swimmer, so I was used to seeing athletes in tight shorts but walking into an emergency room and seeing two grown men in biker shorts really caught me off guard. I met up with dad's friends that he was riding with as well as my mom and sister. We were all standing there waiting to be cleared to go back and see him. In the meantime, the doctors were asking many questions but could not give us many answers. After what seemed like hours, we were able to be back with dad. I remember walking back to the sixth ER room and opening the curtain to see him. When I got to his bedside, I saw dad and his blank face staring at us in almost confusion.

Growing up my dad was always by my side with everything I did. There are so many incredible moments that we shared in the 19 years that I looked up to him. One day that dad and I almost always shared were Sundays. We were usually travelling across the state for my swim meets. It was always an early morning wakeup and getting home after dinner time. During these times I didn't realize it but looking back, I think these were the days we shared most of our memories. From eating at the Denny's in Dale, Indiana on every trip back from Evansville and to scaring him thinking that a snake got in our car during the drive, these were both things

I would never forget. But there was one memory that always makes me smile when I think about it. Back when I was in middle school, dad would take me to swim practice almost every day. This was a time for dad and me to do things that mom probably wasn't supposed to know about. Our favorite rule to break was jamming to Rollin' by Limp Bizkit. I walked into practice every day thinking that I was the man and was ready for anything. I knew I had my dad there to back me up if I needed him. He truly was my rock growing up and learned so many lessons from him.

When dad got moved up to the Trauma unit, I knew that things were going to get better. He was going to get the care that he needed. When I looked at my dad, I saw something that I never saw before, my dad was so vulnerable and couldn't do anything about it. At the time it was out of his hands. It was then when I started to get scared that I would never have my dad back. It took me some time to process everything and realize that we were going to have to step up as a family and be there for each other and most importantly my dad. Yes, the nights in the hospital were rough but remembering all the hard work and long nights my dad did for me to have what I had made it seem like nothing. My dad gave me the best growing up, and I knew I had to try and give that back to him.

Those two months went by fast as I was going through the motions trying to prepare myself for leaving for my freshman year at Indiana State University. It was tough saying goodbye to my parents, but I knew they were going to be there for each other and had a great support system back home. It took myself moving away from my parents to realize that my dad wasn't just my dad. He was my best friend and had actual needs from others around him which I had never thought of before. I know that my mom was going to have to be his round-the-clock caretaker, so I tried to go home as much as I could to help where I could. I feel like through this our family became closer than it had ever been before. Out of all the confusion, anger, and sadness I still saw some light in the situation.

Our family was working as a team to keep everything in line, but I knew in the back of my head that it would've been harder to do if my dad didn't have the mental drive that he had. He always saw the light at the end of the tunnel and did everything to his power to get to that goal. My dad always pushed his body to the max when he was training for his Ironman's and marathons, so I knew he knew how to control his mind and keep pushing. I never questioned my dad's ability to get back to where he was before the accident. It seemed like every week I was getting an update of him standing for so long or walking however many yards around the therapy building. He never ceased to amaze me with his want to be better.

Looking back at my dad's recovery I see all the hard work and dedication that he's put back into himself. It seems that it's been a long road but in the grand scheme of things it's just getting started and he has so much farther to go. When I think about our lives now, I find myself questioning how different our lives would be if his accident would have never happened. But I stop myself every time and think about how many good memories we've made after his accident and were going to have many more. Things still seem very different, but I know that my dad is still the hero I learned to know and love my whole life. I can't wait to see how far he comes in his recovery and bounces back into his normal life like nothing happened. I hope to be half the role model, hero, and best friend my dad was to me, to my kids.

Great memories from a past vacation with the
family – Drake, Dave, and Morgan.

Keep Moving Forward!

CHAPTER SEVEN
Keep Moving Forward

What do I say after all of this? I pause and wonder. Then the phrase, "Keep Moving Forward" continually rings in my ear. No matter the obstacles, I have learned to keep moving forward. That is my mantra and daily motivation. I share it with myself first then with others. This is what I want you to gain from reading this book.

As we continue each day, I feel like we are in the final stretch of the race. Every day is a different challenge. When we left the hospital three years ago, we had no idea the changes that we have had to overcome. Such as changes needed to the house, traveling, leaving the house in general, and not being in a hurry. Packing is now a challenge. You can't just leave spontaneously. Everything must be planned out now. I am like an infant and not really knowing what to expect when being away from the house. With all the medications, supplies, and equipment we must be extremely diligent.

I used to love to cook. Stacy doesn't like it at all but has taken over that roll. I feel horrible not being able to help around the house. It makes me want to push a little more. Finding adaptive equipment should help me help her around the house. This stuff is hard to find. I used to love driving. On my one-year rebirthday, Stacy took me up to the crash site. It was weird, the feelings that came back. She drove back up the hill for a second time. I remember telling her the scenario and what I was feeling at the time.

I will relieve Stacy of that duty someday. She drives everywhere right now. These are my goals for the future. Today I have major anxiety with hospital stays. I remember feeling alone, trapped, and lying in bed counting ceiling tiles. This brings back all the trauma from my accident. I will continue to work on this and determine ways to coupe. As I think back from the beginning of this accident, I cannot thank everyone enough for all the support for me and my family. The staff never once asked them to leave, remember this was the ICU. They would keep saying, "boy, do you have a lot of support."

People still help with lunch to this day. Friends are still willing to help us with anything we need. All we have to do is ask. Sometimes asking is the hardest part. I've learned to swallow my pride and ask. Absolute strangers will help. I'm grateful when they help. Not only did they help me, but it might make their day being able to do something for someone.

Success doesn't happen every day. Some days I feel like I'm going backwards. That's ok because tomorrow is another day to try again. I've struggled with wanting to improve by leaps and bounds. I must continue to remind myself, baby steps. It's not a sprint, but a marathon. **KEEP MOVING FORWARD!** No matter how slow, just don't stop! I have been blessed to talk about my journey. It continues to remind me just how far I have come.

I remind myself daily of a conversation I had with a bus driver early in my recovery. I had never seen him before, and he told me he was a pastor. He asked if I believed in God. I said, "of course." He said we live in a microwave society. We want everything immediately. He said you can't rush God's plan but once he starts something, he finishes it. He continued, "Mr. Miller, he isn't finished with you yet!" I believe God put him on that bus that day to remind me again to live a day at a time and keep moving forward.

STAY STRONG EVERYONE!

KEEP MOVING FORWARD!

Dave's Unbreakable Strength Quotes

References:
Coffee Thoughts – Coaching and Motivation [1]
Distant Runners [2]
shelkykerchner.com [3]

Dave finishing his swim at Ironman Muncie.

You never know how strong you are until being strong is your only choice.
Bob Marley

Keep Moving Forward!

Dave after finishing his 1st marathon.

No one ever injured their eyesight by looking on the bright side.

Keep Moving Forward!

Dave and his Louisville Landshark team after
finishing the Ironman Muncie.

**You won't know your limits until you push
yourself past them.**

Keep Moving Forward!

Dave and Stacy out enjoying a bike ride at the
waterfront.

**The task ahead of you is never greater than
the strength within you.**

Keep Moving Forward!

Dave starting the second leg at Ironman Muncie.

Physical strength will get you to the starting line. But mental strength will get you through the finish line.

Keep Moving Forward!

Dave starting the run portion of the Ironman
Muncie, July 2016.

**One day you will thank yourself for never giving
up.**

Keep Moving Forward!

Dave running to the finish line at Ironman Muncie.

My competition is not against the runner next to me. It's against the runner inside me. [2]

Keep Moving Forward!

Dave's medal, bib, and t-shirt from Ironman Muncie.

When you feel like quitting, think about why you started.

Keep Moving Forward!

This picture was the night before Dave's accident from Mt. Saint Francis. It was the last picture taken of him walking his dog, Bentleigh.

You either get bitter or you get better. It's that simple. You either take what has been dealt to you and allow it to make you a better person, or you allow it to tear you down. The choice does not belong to fate, it belongs to you.

Keep Moving Forward!

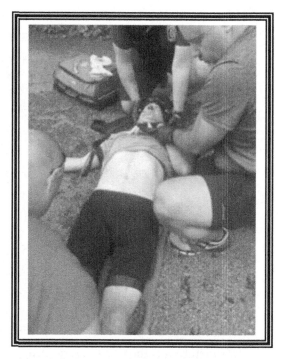

Dave being attended to at the accident by
First Responders.

**The same boiling water that softens the potato
hardens the egg. It's about what you're made of,
not the circumstances.**

Keep Moving Forward!

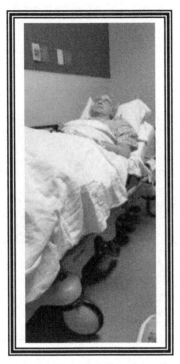

Dave at the hospital before his
hand surgery.

**I am thankful for my struggle because
without it, I wouldn't have stumbled across
my strength!**

Keep Moving Forward!

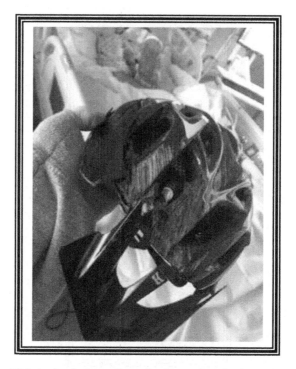

This is the helmet Dave had on when he had the
accident. With only little damage his head remained
safe. The manufacture of the helmet contacted him to
research its engineering structure for future
production innovations.

**Push harder than yesterday if you want a
different tomorrow.**

Keep Moving Forward!

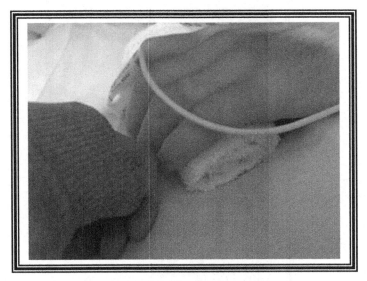

A time for comfort.

Before my accident, my focus was pushing my body beyond its limits. Marathons and triathlons did just that. Now my mind and body are pushed doing daily activities. My goal right after the accident was to hold Stacy's hand and walk down the street. We will accomplish this.

Keep moving forward!

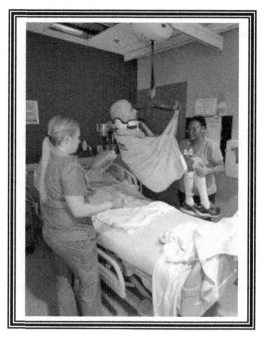

Dave being hoisted with the hoyer to move
to his wheelchair.

**Wake up every day with gratitude. Be
thankful you can feel the floor beneath
your feet. I couldn't for quite some time. I
hope I've become a better man and hope
to inspire others.**

Keep Moving Forward!

On Saturdays and Sundays, Dave would typically not have therapy so Stacy would take him to the gym at Frazier and put him on the bike for extra exercise.

People ask how I stay so positive after losing my legs...I simply ask how they stay so negative with theirs.
Sgt John Joey Jones

Keep Moving Forward!

Dave on the treadmill harnessed in
and ready to go!

Don't tell me you can't!
Juan Jose' Mendez

Keep Moving Forward!

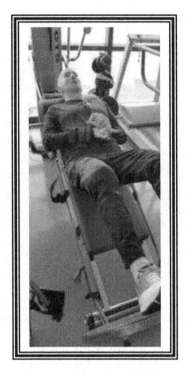

Dave working on rebuilding
strength in his legs and core.

Get in a good workout and...

Keep Moving Forward!

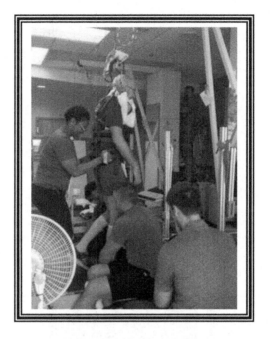

Dave's therapy team assisting on the
treadmill to reteach his body how to walk.

**Being challenged in life is inevitable,
being defeated is optional.**

Keep Moving Forward!

Dave getting stretched out during occupational therapy.

**When you are going through hard times
and wondering where God is, remember
the teacher is always quiet during the test.**

Keep Moving Forward!

The therapist and advocate helping to stabilize Dave's
legs so he can take a step.

**When you have a great support group it
helps you make it.**

Keep Moving Forward!

Dave's first time standing alone at
home.

Getting Stronger!

Keep Moving Forward!

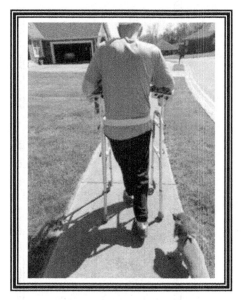

Dave's home advocate, Murphy,
helping with outside walks. He is
Dave's protector and always follows
him to make sure he is ok. We call him
Mayor Murph!

The only disability in life is a bad attitude.

Keep Moving Forward!

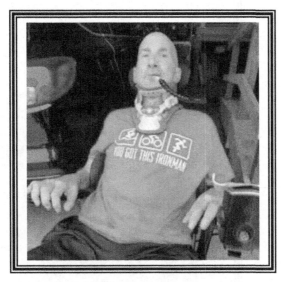

Dave enjoying a nice day outside in the fall of 2017.

Talk about your blessings more than you talk about your burdens.

Keep Moving Forward!

Dave and the family at the fall fundraiser.

**Winners are not people who never fail.
Winners are people who never quit.**

Keep Moving Forward!

The family – Morgan, Stacy, Dave, and Drake

In the family there is a strength that all the power in the world can't undo.

Keep Moving Forward!

Dave's new ride – GRIT Freedom Chair. Stacy applied
for a grant from CFA (Challenge Athlete Foundation).
Dave is now a promoter for the company.

**Sometimes you must let go of the picture of
what you thought your life would look like and
learn to find joy in the story you are living.**

Keep Moving Forward!

Dave doing what he enjoys. He shared his story with the New Albany Boys' Basketball Team State Champs. Go Dogs!

The strength of individual greatness makes a great team.
Lailah Gifty Akita

Keep Moving Forward!

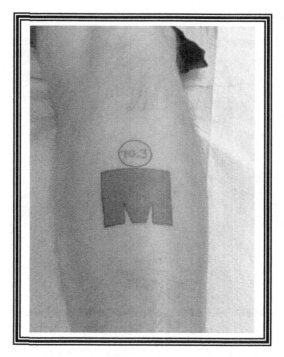

The proof is in the tattoo! Dave got this after he
completed Ironman Muncie. He left the circle open to
fill in after finishing Ironman Louisville. He thinks he
should fill the head in green now to promote spinal
cord awareness.

**If you can't do great things, do small things in
a great way.**

Keep Moving Forward!

Dave seeing the finish line.

It comes down to one simple thing:
How bad do you want it? [1]

Keep Moving Forward!

Connect with Dave Miller

Inspirational Speaker & Force of Positive Endurance

Email: ironcladjourney@gmail.com

Facebook: Dave Miller

Instagram: @conquering_paralysis

Phone: 502-821-9141

Made in the USA
Monee, IL
09 July 2021